DOG BREEDS

Dachshunds

by Sara Green

Consultant:
Michael Leuthner, D.V.M.
PetCare Clinic, Madison, Wisc.

BLASTOFF! READERS
4

BELLWETHER MEDIA · MINNEAPOLIS, MN

Note to Librarians, Teachers, and Parents:

Blastoff! Readers are carefully developed by literacy experts and combine standards-based content with developmentally appropriate text.

Level 1 provides the most support through repetition of high-frequency words, light text, predictable sentence patterns, and strong visual support.

Level 2 offers early readers a bit more challenge through varied simple sentences, increased text load, and less repetition of high-frequency words.

Level 3 advances early-fluent readers toward fluency through increased text and concept load, less reliance on visuals, longer sentences, and more literary language.

Level 4 builds reading stamina by providing more text per page, increased use of punctuation, greater variation in sentence patterns, and increasingly challenging vocabulary.

Level 5 encourages children to move from "learning to read" to "reading to learn" by providing even more text, varied writing styles, and less familiar topics.

Whichever book is right for your reader, Blastoff! Readers are the perfect books to build confidence and encourage a love of reading that will last a lifetime!

This edition first published in 2009 by Bellwether Media.

No part of this publication may be reproduced in whole or in part without written permission of the publisher. For information regarding permission, write to Bellwether Media Inc., Attention: Permissions Department, Post Office Box 19349, Minneapolis, MN 55419-0349.

Library of Congress Cataloging-in-Publication Data
Green, Sara, 1964-
  Dachshunds / by Sara Green.
    p. cm. – (Blastoff! readers. Dog breeds)
  Includes bibliographical references and index.
  Summary: "Simple text and full color photographs introduce beginning readers to the characteristics of the dog breed Dachshunds . Developed by literacy experts for students in kindergarten through third grade"–Provided by publisher.
  ISBN-13: 978-1-60014-218-5 (hardcover : alk. paper)
  ISBN-10: 1-60014-218-4 (hardcover : alk. paper)
  1. Dachshunds–Juvenile literature. I. Title.

SF429.D25G69 2008
636.753'8–dc22   2008019994

Text copyright © 2009 by Bellwether Media, Inc. BLASTOFF! READERS and associated logos are trademarks and/or registered trademarks of Bellwether Media Inc.

SCHOLASTIC, CHILDREN'S PRESS, and associated logos are trademarks and/or registered trademarks of Scholastic Inc. Printed in the United States of America.

NIAGARA FALLS PUBLIC LIBRARY

Contents

What Are Dachshunds?

Dachshunds are long dogs with short legs. Some people call them wiener dogs or hot dogs. Dachshunds are **scent hounds**. They have an excellent sense of smell.

4

Dachshunds come in two sizes. They are **standard** and **miniature**. A standard Dachshund weighs 16 to 28 pounds (7 to 12.7 kilograms). Miniature Dachshunds weigh less than 11 pounds (5 kilograms).

Short-haired Dachshund

fun fact

Wire-haired Dachshunds look very different from Short-haired and Long-haired Dachshunds. Because of this, some people confuse Wire-haired Dachshunds with other breeds of dogs.

Long-haired Dachshund

Dachshund **coats** come in three types. They are Short-haired, Long-haired and **Wire-haired**. The Short-haired Dachshund is the most common type. The Wire-haired Dachshund is the least common.

Dachshund coats come in many colors. They are usually black and tan or red in color. Dachshunds can also be gray, brown and tan, or **dappled** in color.

Wire-haired Dachshund

History of Dachshunds

Dachshunds are originally from Germany. The **breed** has been around for at least 600 years. Its **ancestors** are short dogs called Teckels and hunting dogs called St. Hubert Hounds. The puppies of these two breeds were the first Dachshunds.

The first Dachshunds hunted badgers and other animals that live underground. The name Dachshund means *badger dog* in German.

Early Dachshunds were larger than many of the Dachshunds today. They weighed 30 to 40 pounds (13.5 to 18 kilograms). These large Dachshunds were good at hunting badgers.

Badgers weigh about 35 pounds (16 kilograms). They are strong fighters with sharp teeth. Later, smaller Dachshunds were better for hunting smaller animals such as rabbits and weasels.

A Dachshund's body was perfect for hunting animals that lived underground. Its short, strong legs were good for digging holes to find animals. A Dachshund's long body easily fit into holes. Its loud bark alerted people when it found an animal.

! fun fact

A Dachshund was the very first Olympic mascot. His name was Waldi. He appeared in the 1972 Olympics in Germany.

Even its long tail came in handy. Sometimes Dachshunds got stuck in holes. People rescued Dachshunds by pulling them out of holes by their long tails.

Dachshunds Today

People do not use Dachshunds for hunting anymore. Today they are very popular pets. Dachshunds are full of energy. They love to chase squeaky toys and balls. These activities are similar to the way that earlier Dachshunds chased small animals.

Dachshunds still like to dig holes and bark loudly. However, they can be trained to control these behaviors.

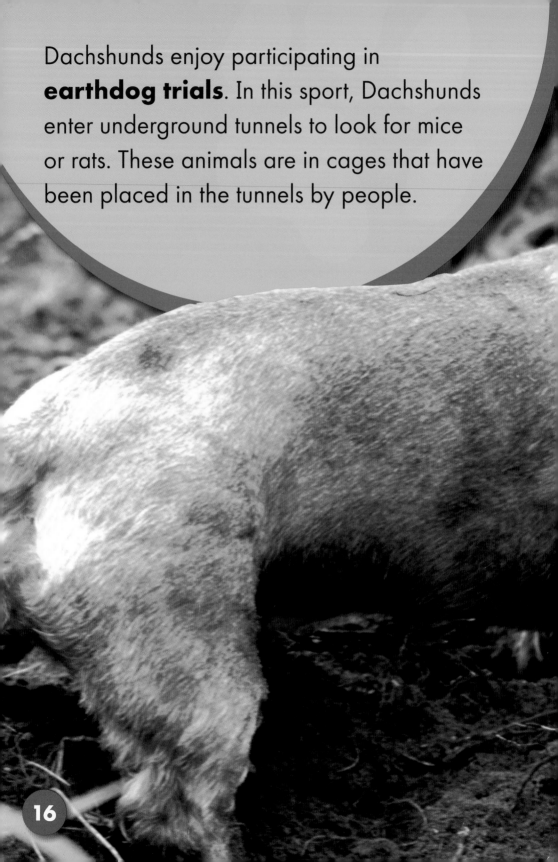

Dachshunds enjoy participating in **earthdog trials**. In this sport, Dachshunds enter underground tunnels to look for mice or rats. These animals are in cages that have been placed in the tunnels by people.

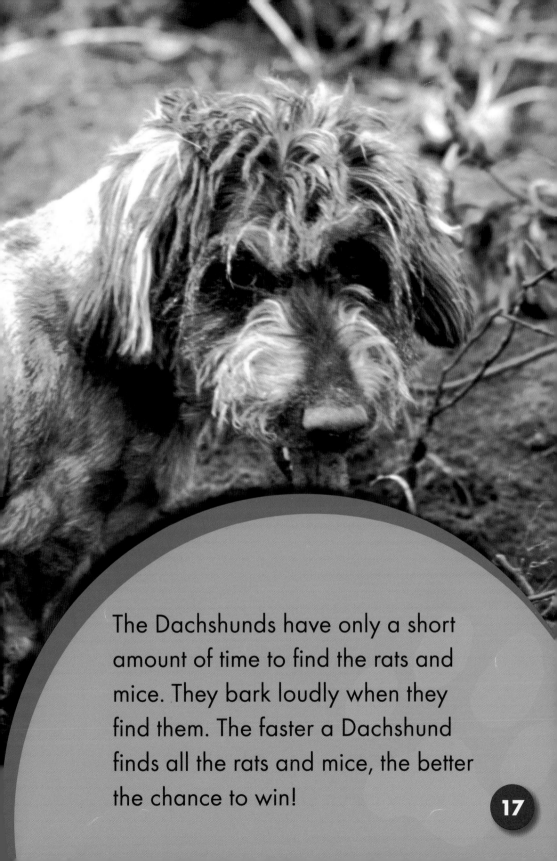

The Dachshunds have only a short amount of time to find the rats and mice. They bark loudly when they find them. The faster a Dachshund finds all the rats and mice, the better the chance to win!

A Dachshund's **spine** can get hurt easily because it is so long. Dachshunds should not jump from even a few feet up. A bad landing can severely hurt a Dachshund's spine.

Staircases can be tough on Dachshunds too. Many people carry their Dachsunds up and down the stairs.

Dachshunds can make great pets. Sometimes they will want to snuggle with people. Other times they will want to dig and play. Dachshunds are friendly pets that are fun to have around.

fun fact

Dachshunds with light-colored coats often have blue or green eyes. They can also have one of each.

Glossary

ancestor—a family member who lived long ago

breed—a type of dog

coat—the hair or fur of an animal

dappled—a coat with spots that are different colors than the background color

earthdog trials—a sport in which dogs search for animals hidden in underground tunnels

miniature size—smaller than standard size

scent hound—a dog that uses its sense of smell to locate things

spine—backbone

standard size—the size within a breed that sets the basis for comparing other sizes

wire-haired—a coat that is made up of coarse, stiff hairs

To Learn More

AT THE LIBRARY

Gray, Susan Heinrichs. *Dachshunds*. Chanhassen, Minn.: Child's World, 2008.

Kallen, Stuart A. *Dachshunds*. Edina, Minn.: Abdo, 1998.

Trumbauer, Lisa. *Dachshunds*. Mankato, Minn.: Coughlan, 2006.

ON THE WEB

Learning more about Dachshunds is as easy as 1, 2, 3.

1. Go to www.factsurfer.com

2. Enter "Dachshunds" into search box.

3. Click the "Surf" button and you will see a list of related web sites.

With factsurfer.com, finding more information is just a click away.

Index

The images in this book are reproduced through the courtesy of: Eric Isselee, front cover; Anna Utekhina, pp. 4-5; imagebroker / Alamy, p. 6; WILDLIFE GmbH / Alamy, p. 6; f1 online / Alamy, p. 7; Mark Raycroft / Getty Images, p. 8; Top-Pics TBK / Alamy, p. 9; tbkmedia.de / Alamy, p. 10; Dan Bannister / Alamy, p. 11; Pix 'n Pages, p. 12-13; Juniors Bildarchiv / Alamy, p. 14; matteo taverna, p. 15; Marga Werner / agefotostock, pp. 16-17; Arco Images GmbH / Alamy, p. 18; Mike Panic, p. 19; Anna Chelnokova, p. 21.

NIAGARA FALLS

FEB 1 4 2009